LESSON 6/

OVERCOMING DEMONIC DREAMS & SPIRIT SPOUSES

With You Tube Audio link

HLOMPHO PHAMODI

OVERCOMING DEMONIC DREAMS & SPIRIT SPOUSES

LESSON 6/ WEEK 6 OF 8

By
©Pastor Hlompho Phamodi
Copyright 2016

LISTEN TO THE AUDIO ON **YOUTUBE** FOR PRAYER GUIDANCE!

https://youtu.be/hj9rXWzU5EA

Watch, Subscribe & Like our YOUTUBE CHANNEL

https://www.youtube.com/channel/UClCWalorVJuSDug8Dc5NOTQ

Follow and like my Facebook page

https://www.facebook.com/hphamodi/

This book is a publication of
HLOMPHO PHAMODI PUBLICATIONS
Cape Town, Western Cape, South Africa
Email: **hlomph@hotmail.com**
Contact No: +27 83 754 1746

Before we start let me pray for you;

> *"Father in the Name of Jesus Christ, Holy Spirit touch Your sons and daughters now in Jesus name. As they read through this book, let them feel your fire and your presence in their spirit, soul and entire body. Let the bound be set free, let the sick be healed in Jesus Name. Thank you Lord that whoever reads this words will experience the fire and touch of God that will turn their lives around and wherever this book goes; there, deliverance will go, power will go, healing will go, provision will go, breakthrough will go, no one will read this book and remain the same. Your divine protection and Angelic ministry be with them all, I decree and prophecy upon their lives that they will not only be transformed by this book but they will be mightily used by God, in the mighty Name of Jesus Christ. Amen."*

The Lord spoke to me about putting together this material to walk a road with you in these 8 weeks; mentoring, coaching and praying with you for total deliverance, healing and restoration in your life and family. May you experience Him like never before. I am praying daily for you and I believe God will meet all your needs. Expect permanent breakthroughs and change in Jesus name.

Pastor Hlompho Phamodi
His Grace Family Church, Cape Town
January 2017
'Through knowledge shall the Just be delivered. Proverbs 11:9b'

TABLE OF CONTENTS

LETS PRAY _____ 3

EVERYTHING BEGINS IN THE SPIRIT_____ 6

WHAT ARE DREAMS _____ 8

IGNORANCE _____ 9

DREAMS FROM THE DEVIL_____ 10

DREAMS ARE A MIRROR _____ 11

DREAM ATTACKS ARE DESIGNED FOR AN INDIVIDUAL _____ 12

CAUSES OF DEMONIC DREAMS _____ 12

DREAM CALENDER _____ 13

DREAM ROBBERS ATTACK _____ 14

LOSS OF SPIRITUAL APPETITE DREAM ATTACK_____ 15

SPIRIT OF DEATH OR UNTIMELY DEATH DREAM ATTACK _____ 15

WHEN YOU DREAM OF A DEAD RELATIVE/PERSONS _____ 17

DEMOTION DREAMS ATTACK _____ 18

FAMILY CURSES DREAM ATTACK_____ 19

FINANCIAL ROBBERS DREAM ATTACK_____ 20

EVIL MONITIRING SPIRITS DREAM ATTACKS _____ 21

SPIRIT OF INFIRMITY (SICKNESS DREAM ATTACKS) _____ 21

EVIL PATTERNS DREAM ATTACK _____ 22

SPIRIT OF STAGNATION DREAM ATTACK _____ 22

SPIRITUAL SPOUSES DREAM ATTACK _____ 23

RENUNCIATION PRAYERS DAY_____ 25

HOW TO BREAK DEMONIC DREAMS _____ 28

ABOUT THE AUTHOR _____ 30

It is said; *everything is spiritual and everything is conceived in the spirit before it's in the natural.* There can be no physical manifestation without a spiritual input. The first time I heard this saying; I questioned it for years but the day God opened my eyes to the spiritual realm I understood it. Now think about it, everything that we are, the world is and how it came about its all from an unseen world. The very thoughts in your mind that are followed by your actions and life is all from within. When we speak about spiritual warfare, we have to acknowledge this truth. When it comes to demonic dreams as we will discuss in this book it's all about **programming from the spiritual realm through your dreams into your life.**

Let me tell you a true story; I counselled a brother the other day that told me whenever he had a sexual dream, the day following the dream will be his worst, he will struggle to pray and be faithful to God. Now the dream was where it all began, the devil drains a lot of people's virtue and anointing through dreams. Some people eat or drink somethings in the dream and they wake up tired and confused.

BEFORE A PERSON IS SICK OR DIES IN THE PHYSICAL THEY FIRST DIE SPIRTUALLY:

A lady from Kenya shared with us how she experienced the spirit of death; she said a lot of times a person will first be killed in the spirit before the natural. I came across a testimony of an ex-Satanists who said that there are mirrors that are used to kill and destroy lives in the kingdom of darkness. What Satanists will do they will call someone's name and if that person appears in the mirror they will stab them on the mirror and sometimes immediately or later that person will die strangely.

- **I declare over your life that every satanic mirror and assembly calling your name to be shattered and destroyed by the FIRE of the HOLY GHOST NOW IN JESUS NAME;**

- **THEY WILL LOOOK FOR YOU, BUT NOT FIND YOU. You will be invisible to the kingdom of darkness in Jesus name. Every untimely death, sickness or accident released in the sprit realm against your life or family members we reverse it now and declare let it go back to the sender in Jesus name.**

The devil understands that before anything manifests in your physical world, it first has to be birthed in the spirit. He actually just uses what GOD has already designed or created. My spiritual father once said this and it changed my life; the devil is a spirit being and knows and sees what is happening in the spirit, hence sometimes before a person gets a breakthrough the devil will send an attack or a dream so that the person will be dispositioned. We that are in spiritual warfare should always be in our rightful position and persist in prayer. Daniel waited 21 days for his breakthrough that was due from day 1, but the Angel said to him the Prince of Persia withstood him all the 21 days. Be aware of the spiritual meanings of everything around you, enjoy your life that is lived in the physical world, but apply your spirit senses to life around you, including your dreams.

It is said that; human beings spend most of their life dreaming, in fact statistics show that by the age of 60 years, you would have spent 20 years of your live dreaming. Meaning 1/3rd *of your life is just spend on dreams. So what are dreams?*

- **Dreams according to Gods plan were designed to convey a divine message from God to man.** Job 33:15-16 explains this; *In a dream, in a vision of the night, when deep sleep falls upon men, while slumbering on their beds. Then He opens their ears of men, and seal instruction.*

- Dreams are a natural way in which the spirit world is open to the natural.

- Dreams are a channel or means of communicating from the supernatural world into the natural.

- Dreams are a doorway into the destiny of man.

- Dreams are a Godly natural way that God has set to speak to man, **but is also being used by the devil to manipulate and program all kinds of evil to man.**

Dreams being a spiritual channel are therefore timeless, for there is no time or distance in the spirit realm. **This explains why someone can dream of a future event before it happens.** We live in a spirit filled world, where the devil is mastered one of the ways to destroy people, especially Gods people. I don't know how many times during a counselling session have I traced a problem of a person to a dream they had. It's time to learn to guard your dream life and to *read/ interpret/discern* dreams in order for you to have victory in live.

IGNORANCE

A lot of believers are so ignorant of the power behind a dream, recently I was invited to speak in a local Christian radio station and I was amazed by the amount of Christians who had dream attacks and all kinds of problems related to dreams. **I soon noticed that the devil is deceived so many people into thinking that they are just merely dreaming, whilst he is busy programming witchcraft, sickness, bondages, poverty and all manner of disaster in their lives.** God says; His people are destroyed for lack of knowledge. You cannot afford to sleep and be a playground for demons. It's time to awake spiritually and take charge of your dream life. **And there is no better way to guard against dream attacks other than through midnight prayers. I urge you to rise up in this season and let the devil know that your dreams are not his dumping place.**

MAN WHO FAIL TO DISCERN THE POWER AND THE MYSTERY BEHIND DREAMS WILL SUFFER IN THIS LIFE, THIS IS ONE AREA WHERE THE BODY OF CHRIST HAS NOT VENTURED INTO AND A LOT OF PEOPLE ARE STRUGGLING WITH DREAM ATTACKS AND DREAM INTERPRETATION.

God is the creator of man and as well as dreams, but the devil takes advantage of these area due to open doors as discussed in the previous *LESSON 5*. Nonetheless we are here to equip you so that you will not become a victim of dream attacks. I will be touching on briefly on spirit spouses due to a number of emails and prayer needs related to dream attacks of spirit spouses.

DREAMS FROM THE DEVIL

God designed you and me to have godly dreams, but Satan took advantage of this channel through the fall of man and brought corruption and manipulation. Matt 13:25; *while men slept his enemies came and sowed tares amongst the wheat and went his way.* The sole purpose of the devil is to sow destruction in people's lives through their dreams. He uses dreams to program man and to cage them. **Your dreams are your spiritual mirror.**

Let me give you a true testimony; *for years I used to have a dream where I would be running from my parents' bedroom into my own/ sibling's bedroom. This dream was very scary as the house will be dark and I would be so terrified, sometimes even unable to wake up, the devil was using this dream to put fear in me and for years I struggled to live freely as God intended for me. After being born-again the dream persisted and even more frequently. I started confronting this attack in prayer and I remember one day, it came again, I was suddenly terrified of the darkness in my parent's room and was ready to run for my life. It* *felt like a presence of darkness and fear all at the same time, I* **remember coming to my senses and taking authority within the dream, I looked at the darkness, fear and evil in its face and commanded it to leave in Jesus name, I had never seen such boldness before, but God was answering my prayer.** *I expelled the fear and terror of this evil spirit and it left. I went into my room where I would normally run to and shielded my brothers and sisters. Since that day I never had that dream attack again.*

I had counselled people with all kinds of dream attacks, mostly witchcraft, some will eat in the dream and get sick physically, some will lose their possessions or money in the dream and only to be fired from their workplace or lose something of value in the natural with no explanation to a sudden loss.

DREAMS ARE A MIRRIOR

I know for a fact that if I am dreaming bad or evil dreams I need to check myself spiritually. **Sometimes they are just attacks, but the best way to monitor your walk of faith is to watch your dreams.**

What are you dreaming right now? I also know from experience that the devil can blind a person so that they forget their dreams. So even if you find yourself forgetting your dreams it can be a sign of a demonic manipulation. Naturally you will dream and forget dreams, but we are talking of dream attacks here and I am here to help you discern them and overcome them.

The enemy hates you and me, and will use dreams to corrupt and manipulate man. Matthew 13:25 teaches us this; while men slept, his enemies came and sowed tares amongst the wheat. Note the Bible say; *his enemies*, these were not outsiders but an in-house enemies, who knew exactly when to attack and how. The devil is a cunning creature, and knows exactly what to do and to who. **All spiritual dream attack is tailor made for an individual. In other words, you will dream what is relevant and specific to you.** The devil comes to kill, steal and destroy; we need to stand our ground. Every child of God needs to know that they are not immune to dream attacks, but by the grace of God through prayer and covering the devil has no power to destroy your life. Declare this prayer with me;

➢ *Every dream attack from the kingdom of darkness, I reverse it now in Jesus name.*

CAUSES OF DEMONIC DREAMS

Demonic attack; sometimes the devil will attack you, for a mere fact that you are Gods child, remember there is war in the heavenlies to destroy your life. I always encourage the saints to be militant and prayerful as they are the targets of these evil powers. the Bible says we are in war; it actually calls us soldiers. So there will be attacks from time to time, but we have the authority to resist the devil and he will flee from us, as James says; *'Obey God, resist the devil, and he will flee* *from you'* (James 4:7) So, James is teaching us a two-part remedy. Firstly, you obey God. Second, resist the devil and he will leave you alone.

> **Every dream attack sent to destroy your life; I command it to perish with its sender in Jesus name.**

Open spiritual doors: sometimes dream attacks are due to open doors on believer's side. You need to read through **LESSON 5** to fully understand this. When there is a door for the devil to use, a door can be sin, unforgiveness, evil past covenants, generational curse etc. These doors need you to address them and deal with them. You are called to walk in the light and not darkness. You cannot walk with God and consult any medium, no matter who they are. God is against any other way other than through His Son Jesus Christ. You cannot chase deliverance or blessing using whichever medium suits you. You are called to believe in God through His Son Jesus Christ and to make Him your Lord and Savior, obey His word and by faith receive your needs.

> **I declare every witchcraft power of darkness assigned over my life and household, be roasted now by fire in Jesus name. (REPEAT SEVERAL TIMES)**

DREAM CALENDER

This dream calendar is going to guide you to discern and see what kind of dream attacks you are dealing with. It's only a guide and there are so many other ways or possibilities that the devil can use, but I believe this list of attacks will assist you in prayer and in getting a breakthrough you need.

DREAM ROBBERS ATTACK

The devil is out to kill, steal and destroy; he is after your joy, blessings, health, family and ministry. You need to *pray violently* if you having repeated occurrences of the following;

- ➤ All forms of robbery attack in a dream, e.g. House break-in or snatching or car hijack.
- ➤ You dream of losing important documents, such as an Identity Document/ passport.
- ➤ Nakedness and seeing your clothing removed from you.
- ➤ Living in house without roof.
- ➤ Losing money.
- ➤ Dreaming of lack etc.

Pray these prayers out loud;

- ➤ Evil arrows go back to your sender (x7)
- ➤ Holy Ghost fire consume every dream robber assigned over my life.
- ➤ (Hold your head) and apply the blood of Jesus Christ upon your mind in Jesus name.
- ➤ Every dream robber assigned to steal from me, I bind you in Jesus name and command you to perish in your ways.
- ➤ I command every stolen goods to be turned back to me in Jesus name.

14

LOSS OF SPIRITUAL APPETITE DREAM ATTACK

The devil also uses dreams to lower our spiritual appetite, watch out for the following dreams and pray accordingly:

- ➤ Eating heavy food.
- ➤ Sexual intercourse.
- ➤ Urinating uncontrollably.

Pray out Loud the following;

- ➤ All demonic caterers feeding me demonic food, I command you to catch fire and die in Jesus name.
- ➤ All injecting demons sent to poison me let your own poison destroy you in Jesus name.
- ➤ Arrows of infirmity sent into my body, I sent you back to your sender.
- ➤ In the name of Jesus by fire, by force I recover all my lost appetite for the things of God.
- ➤ I take back every miracle that belongs to me in Jesus name.

SPIRIT OF DEATH OR UNTIMELY DEATH DREAM ATTACK

Any death related dream is not good, and should not be entertained. The devil kills not only physically but spiritually. There are things God has deposited in you that should be born; there is an office in you that should be occupied. **Just as Herod wanted to kill Jesus at his infancy**

15

the devil knowing the office Jesus was going to occupy tried to stop him before his time. Every spirit out there out to kill you before your time, I bind it in the mighty name of Jesus; you shall live and not die.

Some dream manifestations are;

- ➤ Seeing a grave.
- ➤ Seeing a coffin.
- ➤ Seeing being shot or stabbed to death.
- ➤ A relative sent into a mortuary.
- ➤ Singing burial songs.
- ➤ Falling unconsciously.

Read psalms 118:17, and pray aggressively the following;

Pray aggressively for yourself or family/ relative:

- ➤ In the Name of Jesus spirit of death, you shall not harvest my life (x7).
- ➤ Arrows of death you shall not locate me or my family in Jesus name.
- ➤ I break the covenant with death in Jesus name.
- ➤ I bind the spirit of the grave in Jesus name.
- ➤ Any dream of death I have ever heard, either of myself, my family or anyone connected to me, I declare you shall not prosper in Jesus name.
- ➤ Spirit of car accidents I declare you will not harvest my life.
- ➤ Infirmities and inherited life threatening diseases, you are not my portion in Jesus name.
- ➤ Cycles of pain and death, BREAK in the name of Jesus.
- ➤ Gates of death be shut upon my life and family in Jesus name.

> I will live long, and enjoy the fruits of my labor in Jesus name.

NOTE: AS A BORN-AGAIN CHRISTIAN YOU ARE NOT SUPPOSED TO DREAM OF DEAD PEOPLE IN ANY WAY. IT'S A DEMONIC CHANNEL THAT THE DEVIL IS USING TO INTRODUCE YOU TO DEMONIC PRACTICES SUCH AS NECROMANCY PRACTICES OR ANCESTRAL WORSHIP.

WHEN YOU DREAM OF A DEAD RELATIVE/PERSONS

Pray this prayer and if needed take a 3-day fasting if the dreams still persist;

> Every door, spiritual eye or third eye opened to see the dead spirits; I command it to close now in Jesus name.
> Lord I will only see what the Holy Spirit wants me to see and not the evil spirits.
> I cancel every initiation declared upon my life that is a result of this dreams.
> I renounce every involvement with the dead in any way.
> I cleanse my dreams with the blood of Jesus and let go of any sorrow, guilt or ill feelings for the departed loved once.
> In Jesus name I receive deliverance in this area amen.

The devil ultimately wants to shame you. He wants you to lose confidence in God; He wants you to be demoted so you can say there is no God,

Here are some dream manifestations;

- Seeing yourself doing a job below your standard.
- Seeing yourself in a small house.
- Seeing yourself being fired from work.
- Seeing people conspiring about your demotion.
- Seeing people plotting your demotion.
- Begging for money in dream.

Pray these strategic prayers;

- Any demoting household spirits I command you to bypass me in Jesus name.
- Arrows of shame and disgrace; what are you waiting for, back to the sender in Jesus name.
- I blot out with the blood of Jesus every demoting dream in Jesus name.
- Any garments of shame, demotion and stagnation forced upon me, tear and catch fire now in Jesus name.
- Lord by your mercy, turn my demotion into promotion.
- Lord turn my shame to fame.
- Anointing of double honor, manifest in my life for all to see.

> Dream of rise and fall projected against me be destroyed by fire in Jesus name.

FAMILY CURSES DREAM ATTACK

The devil uses family curses sometimes to try and cage people, even Christians. Most of us come from backgrounds where our families or parents consulted mediums, familiar spirits and sangomas (witch doctors). You have accepted the Lord but never broke that generational curse, and in the spirit realm contracts speak. As long as that contract is still tied to your name you will have difficulties.

Some dream manifestations are;

> Seeing old dead relatives.
> Contracts that bear your name.
> Meetings where you are discussed.
> Evil items in your possession.

Strategic prayers are;

> Confess all known and unknown generational curse, cover everything under the Blood of Jesus.
> You arrows of generational curses break now in Jesus name.
> I command every evil spirit of generational curse in my life to be broken now in Jesus name.
> I release my destiny from any ancestral curse working against my destiny.
> All dead relatives, familiar spirits in my family I block your assignment in the name of Jesus.

19

You labor a lot, but reap nothing; Haggai 1: 6, 8-9, 11. The Lord wants me to tell you that it's time to break free out of poverty, out of debts and out of financial limitations.

Dream manifestation may include;

> ➢ Putting money in your pocket, filled with holes.
> ➢ Being robbed of money in dream.
> ➢ Seeing yourself begging, in lack or destitute.
> ➢ Exchanging money in dream.

Confession and Repentance;

> ➢ *Confess every disobedience and unfaithfulness in tithing and giving.*

And Pray;

> ➢ Spirit of poverty manifesting in my dreams I command you to be destroyed in Jesus name.
> ➢ Any curse that makes me to gather into a bag full of holes I cancel it now in the name of Jesus.

You need to deal ruthlessly with evil monitoring spirits if you are experiencing the following;

- Seeing strange bird following you in the natural or in a dream.
- Seeing strange eyes in dream or natural.
- Seeing a fly following you.
- Hearing strange movements following you.
- Dreaming of a house without windows or doors.

Prayers;

- Any witchcraft satellite erected to monitor my progress, collapse in Jesus name.
- I destroy every in-house monitoring spirits, planted by the enemy in my house.

SPIRIT OF INFIRMITY (SICKNESS DREAM ATTACKS)

Have you ever gone to bed well and woke up sick, this is a sign of a dream attack in the area of your health;

Pray;

- Spirit of infirmity you are not my portion I bind you in Jesus name.
- Demonic sickness I command you to leave my body with all your possessions now in Jesus name.
- I break the spirit of sickness in Jesus name.
- By His stripes I am healed and delivered in Jesus name.

21

Yoke of evil family patterns is a uniform problem in a family linage; it is also called a yoke of collective captivity. **It is the battle your father or mother fought and is now facing you.**

Dream manifestation;

- ➤ Seeing yourself and your dead father/mother always together.
- ➤ Seeing yourself divorced.
- ➤ Seeing yourself back where you come from.
- ➤ Always late for meetings.

Pray;

- ➤ Yoke of collective captivity and non-achievement in my life break and release me in Jesus name.
- ➤ Yoke of collective captivity of no promotion and late graduation break and release me.
- ➤ I declare I am a curse breaker and I will not be bound by what bound my parents.

SPIRIT OF STAGNATION DREAM ATTACK

This is a terrible spirit, if the devil cannot stop you from getting to your promised land, he will delay you, just as he did with Israel in the wilderness. Deuteronomy 2: 1-3

Any dreams where you see the following;

- ➤ Going in circles, perhaps walking or driving.
- ➤ Seeing the same things over and over while you walk.
- ➤ Feeling caged, or limited.
- ➤ Your feet stuck in mud.

Pray;

- ➤ Spirit of stagnation, I command you to loose me and let me go.
- ➤ Any agent of darkness assigned to delay my breakthrough catch fire and die in Jesus name.
- ➤ I receive total deliverance from dream attacks in Jesus name.

SPIRITUAL SPOUSES DREAM ATTACK

Any dream where you dream having sex is a sign of a spirit spouse attack. This is one area where you don't want to relax. A lot of believers are struggling in areas such as:

- ➤ Hatred of marriage or your husband/wife
- ➤ Difficulty in getting married
- ➤ Difficulty in having children
- ➤ Menstrual cycle problems
- ➤ Having a miscarriage after a sexual dream
- ➤ Impotence/ loss of sexual drive for man
- ➤ Financial lack and failure at edge of breakthrough
- ➤ Inability to maintain a holy lifestyle
- ➤ Unexplainable problems, delays and failures in life.

This is an operation of the spirit spouse. There is no need to be ashamed. A lot of believers struggle silently with this problem, sometimes the spirit spouse can also hide, let us discuss the different types of spirit spouses:

1. **Hidden spiritual spouse**; This are people who don't know they have a spouse in the spirit, as soon as they finish dreaming the demon deletes the dream in their minds. Have you ever dreamed and you woke up having forgotten what you dreamed; pray about it, it is not normal. This is a very dangerous place to be because you are not sure what's going on, *but in the name of Jesus every hidden dream will be exposed tonight in Jesus name.*

2. **Camouflaged spirit spouse**; this is a spirit spouse that uses someone's face to trick you into sex in a dream. This person can be innocent and know nothing about your experience. The realm of fantasy is demonic and can often lead into these kind of dream, so it's important to not entertain fantasy thoughts, even if you are engaged to be married to someone, you are not permitted to fantasy about having sex with them until you are married. Your mind controls your world. You are in control of your mind so use it for the glory of God.

3. **Manifest spirit spouse**; this spouse is literally a man or a woman. A woman once visited a pastor for counselling and immediately started to have dreams about this pastor. She reported as seeing the pastor appearing in her dreams to sleep with her and telling her that he swims inside of her every night. It didn't take long the lady actually started an affair with the same pastor, she was married and her marriage collapsed suddenly. She ended up bound to this ungodly man day and

night, only to find out that he wasn't really a pastor but was a Satanist. So people can have real human beings spirit spouses. Satanist can astral project and sleep with people in their dreams. In Africa there are stories of 'tokoloshe' (a dwarf- like water spirit manifest as a man) is known to rape and molest woman. This spirit also acts as a spouse.

4. **Generational spirit spouse**; through parents these spirits can be passed on to the next generation. In most African countries these spirits are acknowledged and worshiped, they are the gods over families and own those families; no matter who gets born they are initiated and married to this demon from birth.

5. **Territorial Spirit spouse**; places have been reported of being owned by these strongman, every woman in that village is married to this one spirit spouse and in most cases these women are very immoral or filled with prostitution.

RENUNCIATION PRAYERS DAY

1. I resign my involvement in any way from spiritual spouse altars. I withdraw any part of my body and blood deposited on these altars in Jesus name.
2. I withdraw my pictures, images and inner man from the altars in the sea and covens of evil association in Jesus name.

3. I purge myself of all evil sperm in my system from evil associations.

4. I break all inherited covenants with marine spirits.
5. I renounce and divorce a spiritual husband/wife, I declare I am no longer yours, I belong to Christ and I break my covenant with you now in Jesus name.
6. I break any soul ties with marine friends or associations.
7. I claim back from Satan and all the marine kingdom, my earthly belongings in the custody of the spirit husband/wife.
8. Spirit husband/ wife Let me LOOSE BY FIRE, in the name of Jesus.
9. Spirit husband/wife, I DIVORSE you by the POWER OF THE BLOOD OF JESUS.
10. Every spirit wife/ husband I command you to DIE AND NEVER RISE AGAIN, in the name of Jesus.
11. EVERYTHING you have deposited in my life, let it come out now by fire, in the name of Jesus.
12. Every ASSEMBLY that is working against my marriage, be destroyed, in the name of Jesus.
13. I divorce and renounce my marriage with the spirit husband or wife, in the name of Jesus.
14. I break all covenants entered into by MYSELF OR FAMILY with the spirit husband or wife, in the name of Jesus.
15. *Fire of God to burn to ashes THE WEDDING GOWN, RING, PHOTOGRAPHS AND ALL OTHER MATERIALS USED FOR MY MARRIAGE with spirit spouse, in Jesus' name.*
16. *Fire of God to burn to ashes EVERY MARRIAGE CERTIFICATE, in the name of Jesus. (REPEAT SEVERAL TIMES)*
17. I DESTROY every BLOOD AND SOUL-TIE with the spirit husband/ wife, in the name of Jesus.
18. Fire of God to burn to ashes the CHILDREN BORN TO THIS MARRIAGE, THEY ARE ILLEGAL in Jesus' name.

19. *I WITHDRAW MY BLOOD, SPERM OR ANY OTHER PART OF MY BODY deposited on the altar of the spirit husband or wife, in Jesus name.*

20. You spirit husband/ wife tormenting my life and earthly marriage I BIND YOU IN JESUS NAME AND CAST YOU OUT OF MY LIFE INTO THE DEEP PIT, and I command you not to ever come into my life again, in the name of Jesus.

21. I return to you, EVERY PROPERTY OF YOURS IN MY POSSESSION in the spirit world, including the dowry and whatsoever was used for the marriage and covenants, in the name of Jesus.

22. I DRAIN/ FLUSH MYSELF WITH THE BLOOD OF JESUS of all evil materials deposited in my body as a result of our sexual relation, in Jesus' name.

23. Lord, SEND HOLY GHOST FIRE INTO MY ROOT AND BURN OUT ALL UNCLEAN THINGS deposited in it by the spirit husband or wife, in the name of Jesus.

24. I BREAK AND CRUSH the head of the snake, deposited into my body by the spirit husband /wife to do me harm, and command it to come out, in the name of Jesus.

25. I FLUSH OUT, WITH THE BLOOD OF JESUS, EVERY EVIL MATERIAL/ POISON/ SNAKE deposited in my womb to prevent me from having children on earth.

26. Lord, REPAIR AND RESTORE EVERY DAMAGE done to any part of my body and my earthly marriage by the spirit husband /wife, in the name of Jesus.

27. I REJECT AND CANCEL EVERY GENERATIONAL CURSE, EVIL PRONOUNCEMENT, SPELL, ENCHANTMENT AND INCANTATION place upon me by the spirit husband or wife, in the name of Jesus.

28. I GIVE THANKS for my Deliverance in Jesus name.

1. **Close every evil open door in your life, that are giving the enemy access into your life.** For example, you can remove gossip from your life, if every time you hear some bad information on someone, you must insist on praying for them. The next time a gossiper stops you at your doorstep and has something to say, turn the gossip meeting into a prayer meeting "Oh, that devil sure is hitting our friend hard. Let's pray!" Start the prayer immediately. This is super effective!

2. **Break unhealthy relationships**; Your friends who are leading you astray must go. Those old friends who pull you down, they are a spiritual hindrance in your life, get rid of them. The devil uses ungodly associations to tie so many people. What kind of friends do you have?

3. **Search prayerfully your home for demonic icons**; remember anything that a demon would claim is unholy and can be a contact point for demons to enter your home. Do these exercises prayerful as the Holy Spirit knows best and He will direct you.

'I pray that from today onwards that your dreams will be consecrated unto God, I apply the blood of Jesus upon them now. I decree divine visitation, prophetic dreams to be your portion in Jesus name. I prophecy elevation and advancement upon your live. Every demotion is turned around to promotion. I prophecy health and breakthrough in Jesus name. May your dreams be filled with angelic activity, may you experience Gods divine instructions, guidance and revelation

through your dreams. I believe God is heard your prayers. The name of the Lord be with you. Amen'

Pastor Hlompho Phamodi is a born again, chosen vessel of God, a general and a commander in the Kingdom of God, an anointed man of God who is called to proclaim and demonstrate the Word of God. He is called to pastor, coach and equip the saints in the area of Deliverance, Healing and Spiritual warfare. His preaching's and writings are backed up with signs and wonders to deliver, to heal and set free the captives. He is a man under submission to spiritual authority; he serves under the apostolic covering of Apostle M Oliphant at His Grace Family Church in Cape Town. He is a married to 'Makarabo Phamodi and lives in Cape Town South Africa.

DEDICATION & ACKNOWLEDGEMENT

I will love to dedicate this work to the Most Important Person on this planet and in my life, Jesus Christ, without Him I can do nothing. Without His presence in my life these are just mere words.

To my precious wife, 'Makarabo Phamodi, I thank God for you love and prayers.

To my beloved son Karabo, I bless the Lord for your life, thank you for your inspiration.

To my spiritual parents in the Lord, Apostle and mama Oliphant, thank you for your faith in me.

To my parent's back home in Lesotho, Mr. & Mrs. (Bishop) Phamoli (Senior) I am forever grateful.

To my founding parents in the faith Arc-Bishop Kolisang and mama Bishop Kolisang, I am where I am because of you.

©Pastor Hlompho Phamodi
First Published 2016

Made in the USA
Columbia, SC
05 May 2023

16143650R10019